Sexuality and the Schools

DATE DUE

PRE

The Practicing Administrator's Leadership Series
_____
Jerry J. Herman and Janice L. Herman, Editors

ROADMAPS
TO SUCCESS

Other Titles in This Series Include:

Sexuality and the Schools

Handling the Critical Issues

Joan L. Curcio, Lois F. Berlin
Patricia F. First

CORWIN PRESS, INC.
A Sage Publications Company
Thousand Oaks, California

For information address:

Corwin Press, Inc.
A Sage Publications Company
2455 Teller Road
Thousand Oaks, California 91320

SAGE Publications Ltd.
6 Bonhill Street
London EC2A 4PU
United Kingdom

SAGE Publications India Pvt. Ltd.
M-32 Market
Greater Kailash I
New Delhi 110 048 India

Printed in the United States of America

Library of Congress Cataloging-in-Publication Data

Curcio, Joan L.
    Sexuality and the schools : handling the critical issues / Joan L.
Curcio, Lois F. Berlin, Patricia F. First.
        p.   cm. — (Roadmaps to success)
    Includes bibliographical references (pp. 54-58).
    ISBN 0-8039-6265-7 (pbk.)
    1. Students—United States—Sexual behavior. 2. Sexual ethics—
Study and teaching—United States. 3. Hygiene, Sexual—Study and
teaching—United States. 4. Sexual harassment in education—United
States—Prevention. 5. Sex instuction—United States.   I. Berlin,
Lois F.   II. First, Patricia F.   III. Title.   IV. Series.
HQ27.C87   1996
306.7'07—dc20   95-37402

This book is printed on acid-free paper.

96 97 98 99 00 10 9 8 7 6 5 4 3 2 1

Corwin Press Production Editor: S. Marlene Head

Contents

Foreword

In *Sexuality and the Schools: Handling the Critical Issues,* Joan Curcio, Lois Berlin, and Patricia First have produced a very thoughtful and helpful volume that deals with important and emotionally charged problems faced by all educators in the United States. Six chapters provide clear information for use by educators on the "hot button" issues of partners and pregnancy, HIV and AIDS, gay and lesbian sexuality, sexual harassment and violence, and sex education.

A variety of specialized and helpful features are included:

- Each chapter provides practical background information.
- Legal and policy issues are addressed.
- Moral and ethical issues are discussed.
- An annotated bibliography and complete references are provided.

A copy of this book belongs on every educator's desk as a quick reference guide. Its useful, up-to-date information and clear and concise writing style are indispensable for educators who find themselves on the sex education firing line—and in need of its practical, intelligent advice.

JERRY J. HERMAN
JANICE L. HERMAN
Series Co-Editors

About the Authors

Joan L. Curcio is Associate Professor in the Division of Administrative and Educational Services at Virginia Polytechnic Institute and State University and coordinates graduate programs in educational administration at the university's Northern Virginia Graduate Center near Washington, D.C. Curcio's teaching emphasis and research agenda address the effect of organizational governance and the legal structure of schools on children and the learning environment. She has authored books, monographs, chapters, and articles and presented nationally on the issues of justice and care in schools. She is co-editor with Patricia L. First of a new journal titled *Journal for a Just and Caring Education,* which publishes research and practice on the creation of schools as just and caring communities within the context of a changing society. Curcio has had extensive public school experience as a teacher, assistant principal, high school principal, and assistant superintendent. She was named among the 100 Top Administrators in North America in 1984 by the National School Boards Association for her work as principal.

Lois F. Berlin is the Principal of Jefferson-Houston Elementary School in Alexandria, Virginia. She has had extensive experience as a teacher, special educator, assistant principal, and elementary school principal. She has authored policy for the Virginia Department of Education and presented numerous workshops in the area of special education. Berlin is currently working on her Ph.D. at Virginia Tech.

Patricia F. First is Dean of the School of Education and Professor of Educational Administration at the University of Dayton. She is author of *Educational Policy for School Administrators,* co-editor of *School Boards: Changing Local Control* published in the Contemporary Issues Series of the National Society for the Study of Education, coauthor with Joan L. Curcio of *Violence in the Schools: How to Proactively Prevent and Defuse It* and *Individuals With Disabilities: Implementing the Newest Laws,* and she has published numerous articles in policy and practitioner journals. First has been a teacher and administrator in both K-12 and higher education, a policy analyst with both state and federal government, and a National Education Policy Fellow. She earned her B.S. at the University of Massachusetts and her M.S. and Ed.D. at Illinois State University.

Introduction

If we're not part of the solution, we're part of the problem. We have a moral obligation to act, lest our professions and organizations earn the label immoral.

LAWSON (1995)

Acknowledging the Unthinkable

Traditionally, parents have sent their children off to school every day, confident that teachers will educate them in a caring and safe environment. Most believe that whatever the failings of our schools educationally, children will be cared for and safe from harm. This sense of security has diminished as television and newspapers report daily incidents of sexual harassment, abuse, and assault in and around schools: A gang of boys rapes a high school girl in the school storage closet; a high school drama teacher and coach sexually harasses and molests a series of girls during the course of his career; a middle school student is harassed by her classmates both verbally and with inscriptions on the bathroom wall insinuating her inclination to perform sexual acts with hot dogs; a young female teacher is harassed by male students who comment on her body, her sex life, and ways they can satisfy her sexually; a series of teachers is accused and indicted for fondling and sexually molesting students. Less often reported but just

1

as prevalent in schools are instances of harassment, abuse, and prejudice suffered by students infected with the human immunodeficiency virus (HIV) or have developed acquired immune deficiency syndrome (AIDS), students whose sexual orientation is gay or lesbian, and students who become pregnant.

As educators, we may be reluctant for many reasons to acknowledge that these realities exist in our schools. First and foremost, many administrators and teachers experience discomfort in dealing with sexuality in the school setting. Most have little or no training in what to do or say, who to contact, who to call on in resolving a difficult situation, or how to negotiate sensitive, controversial matters. Also, for complex social reasons, many school officials tend to accept certain aberrant behaviors as normal for children and adults. More than one school administrator has explained boys' teasing and harassing of girls about their bodies or pulling up their skirts, for example, as a case of "boys being boys," rather than acknowledging that such behavior is frequently a prelude to sexual harassment and determining what the school staff's responsibility is to address the behavior. We are reluctant to admit that anything, particularly misconduct of a sexual nature, could be happening in "our" school.

We also are reluctant to confront the sexual harassment or abuse of students by colleagues or employees in schools, as well as other critical sexual issues. It is easier to let difficult issues lie. Unfortunately, inaction contributes to an environment where response to sexual harassment, abuse, or prejudice, or to parental or community concerns about them, is inadequate. Failure to act destroys trust and confidence in the ability of those in charge to provide safe, fair, and equitable schooling for students.

The extent of sexual behavior and its related issues and concerns on school campuses today, according to media reports, research, and our own reflective observations, is on the rise. That reality has to be acknowledged. At the same time, we must acknowledge that there is no other topic in the public schools as likely to be sensitive or emotionally charged for parents, students, and school officials.

Taking the Proactive Approach

It is important that administrators approach the topic of sexuality in a caring, concerned, and ethical manner and that they work with parents to gain the support and guidance that can ensure constructive action. Strategies, guidelines, policies, and constructive attitudes can help school officials fulfill their responsibility to provide a safe and healthy school environment and ultimately enable them to create healthy communities containing healthy schools that educate healthy children: children who are neither perpetrators nor victims of sexual harassment, prejudice, or abuse; children who can grow up to be healthy adults.

As authors, we know and respect these facts: Each school community has its own set of issues, its own set of cultural and community values, and its own unique demographic makeup, all of which will determine what is most or least helpful in what we have to share. However, it is important for us to say that this book is born of real school experiences, real situations, and real dilemmas that bedevil administrators every day. Reaching into our collective experiences in public schools, as well as into the rich literature on the topic that has informed our past research and writings, we have tried to outline problems, describe situations, and articulate ways for school personnel to take the lead in handling proactively, and in the best interests of children, critical issues arising in relation to sexuality and the schools. These issues cry out for ethical and caring solutions by educators so that schools will not be indicted as part of the problem.

Chapters to Come

Although many issues could be defined as sexuality issues, we have chosen five that represent the most pressing in terms of the concern they currently engender among students, parents, teachers, administrators, and the broader community, as well as the attention they have received by the media, the courts, and other social institutions. Those topics are teenage pregnancy, HIV and AIDS, sexual orientation, sexual harassment (from teasing to violence), and sex education. In our view, sexuality in the schools needs to be addressed in a forthright, caring, and intelligent manner, keeping the best interests and health of kids at heart while respecting the diversity of opinions that exists regarding these matters. Chapters 2 through 6 consider the ethical, legal, and policy issues related to each of the five topics and discuss possible approaches to dealing with them.

Searching for Intimacy:
Partners and Pregnancy

Teen pregnancy and childbearing first gained wide recognition as a social problem in the early 1970s. To this day, however, debate continues about the nature of the problem and how questions about it should be framed. Whose problem is it? What exactly is the problem? Is it teens engaging in sexual intercourse? Teens having intercourse outside of marriage? Teens having babies? Teens choosing to rear babies? Teens having abortions? Or is it the rising incidence of these occurrences (Lee & Berman, 1992)? Each of these questions would appear to address only a part of a larger problem to which there is no single answer or solution. The growing incidence of teen pregnancy—"children having children" before they have themselves had the opportunity to grow and fully become independent and strong adults—is rooted in numerous social, psychological, cultural, and economic causes. Just as the causes are multiple, so are the contexts and solutions. The following statistics represent conservative estimates of aspects of the problem (Fischer & Sorenson, 1991):

- More than 1 million American teenage girls become pregnant annually.
- Forty percent of these pregnancies end in abortion, representing about one third of the total legal abortions in the United States.

- Thirty thousand babies are born annually to teenage mothers under the age of 15.
- Approximately 90% of teenage mothers keep their babies; only 8% are put up for adoption.
- Seventy percent of adolescent females and 80% of adolescent males engage in sexual activity sometime during their teens.
- Forty percent of American teenagers—5 million girls and 7 million boys—are sexually active.

Some of the most serious consequences of teenage pregnancy include

- Reduced educational achievement for teenage mothers
- Limited vocational opportunities for women who bear children during their teens
- Larger completed family size for females who have their first baby during their teen years
- Increased individual and social costs
- Health problems for both teenage mothers and their babies

Some of the individual and social costs stem from the fact that teenage pregnancies are more likely to result in low infant birth weight, toxemia, mental retardation, infant mortality, and birth defects than are adult pregnancies.

Overall Moral and Ethical Issues

Children are socialized into sex roles—those of being a "real boy" or a "real girl"—at a very early age. Their understanding of sex roles is influenced, in large part, by socially learned activities and symbols that they use in the formation of their sexual identities. The toys they play with, the clothes they wear, the way they talk and communicate, the friends they choose, and how they express their emotions both reveal and determine who they are. For example, boys are not free to cry or be tender; the most acceptable boy-to-boy physical contact is aggressive, not affectionate. Boys learn to touch girls when no one is looking, take advantage of those who are younger and probably won't tell, and boast about it among their peers. They learn to be unemotional, ungiving, and macho—attributes of "real men." Girls learn social activities that will help them become "real women"— how to be good, obedient, helpful, and not too smart; how to be cooperative and not make trouble; how to be cute and coy to get what they want; how to walk and talk and smile in ways that will earn the approval and admiration of the boys or men in their lives. These roles define for children and early adolescents who does what with whom or to whom, what activities are appropriate and when, and who is in charge. Girls learn to relate to themselves and are related to by others as passive, reactive, cooperative, emotional, and nurturing, whereas boys are regarded as active, competitive, aggressive, rational, and unemotional (LaCerva, 1992).

Just as younger boys and girls learn specific sex roles, there are sharp polarities in the way male and female teenagers tend to approach love and heterosexual relationships. Boys seek variety, and girls want intimacy. The classic formulation still seems to be played out: Girls give sex to get love from boys, and boys give love to get sex from girls. According to one study, more than 60% of sexually experienced girls were going steady with or engaged to their first sexual partners, whereas less than 40% of teenage boys had their first sexual experience with a steady girlfriend or fiancee. Boys were more than twice as likely to have intercourse with someone they had only recently met (Whitehead, 1994).

These gender polarities are most pronounced in early adolescence. Physical changes during puberty carry different psychological meanings for boys and girls. For boys, increases in body weight and size bring an enhanced sense of personal power, dominance, and independence, whereas similar changes in girls frequently lead to uncertainty, anxiety, and feelings of powerlessness. This is how it works for teenage girls: In a society where thin models are admired and very young girls on TV sitcoms fret about whether their looks are pleasing to adolescent boys, weight gain can inspire feelings of fear and self-disgust. These feelings are translated into reality the first time they are teased or set apart because of their developing bodies. It is not surprising that Gilligan (1982) and other researchers have noted a decline in young adolescent girls' feelings of competence and confidence at roughly the same time that adolescent boys are becoming more assertive and cocky.

So what does gender polarity have to do with teenage pregnancy? Just at the time when girls are feeling insecure and boys are feeling ready to sow their oats, teenagers are becoming sexually active, and at increasingly younger ages. In 1970, 5% of 15-year-old girls and 32% of 17-year-old girls reported having had sex; by 1988, the figures had increased to 26% of 15-year-olds and 51% of 17-year-olds. By age 19, nearly 80% of young women have had sexual intercourse. As a result of earlier sexual initiation among girls, the historical gender gap in first sexual experiences is narrowing; according to the 1988 National Survey of Young Men (cited in Whitehead, 1994), one third of teenage males have had sex by age 15 and 86% by age 19. Early initiation also means that today's adolescents have more partners: Among never-married, sexually experienced teenage girls in 1971, 38% had had two or more sexual partners; by 1988, the figure had increased to 59%. And they have sex more frequently: The 1988 National Survey of Family Growth (cited in Whitehead, 1994) reported that 45% of never-married, sexually active girls had intercourse at least once a week, as compared with 40% when the survey was administered in 1982. The largest relative increase in sexual intercourse among teenage girls has occurred among those 15 years of age, from 4.6% in 1970 to 25.6% in 1988.

Unfortunately, teenagers' sense of responsibility and ability to plan for the future often are not commensurate with their sexual sophistication. Only 14% of teenage girls use contraceptives the first time they have intercourse. Most wait until they have been sexually active for 9 months or more before they visit a birth control clinic, and the first visit to the clinic is usually for a pregnancy test (Stark, 1986). These facts may be connected to the passive social role played by many young girls in the United States, a role powerfully described by a now-mature mother of two daughters:

> As a woman, I feel I never understood that I was a person, that I could make decisions and I had a right to make decisions. . . . I still let things happen to me rather than make them happen, than make choices, although I know all about choices. . . . I think that if you don't grow up feeling that you ever have any choices, you don't have the sense that you have emotional responsibility. With this sense of choice comes this sense of responsibility. (Gilligan, 1982, p. 67)

It is not unreasonable to expect schools to share responsibility with parents for providing opportunities for girls and boys to grow in their sense of responsible participation in a larger society. Schools can also encourage adolescents to make independent, healthy choices that provide increasing options as they approach adulthood.

A New View of Traditional Roles

Studies have shown that adolescent girls are more likely to hold traditional views of sex roles; that is, they perceive their relationship to males as submissive, dependent, nurturing, supporting, and cooperating. Michele Fine, who spent a year studying students in a New York City public high school, observed that pregnant students in that school had strongly traditional notions of being female. They did not present themselves as sensual or experienced seducers. To the contrary, they were quiet and passive in class, sitting perfectly mute. "She never disrupts. Never disobeys. Never speaks. And is never identified as a problem" (Fine, in Sadker & Sadker, 1994, p. 119).

Traditional views of sex roles are strongly correlated with lower socioeconomic status and low self-esteem. As Sadker and Sadker (1994) assert, when a girl lives in educational or economic poverty—without respect to her racial or ethnic background—the stage is set for a teenage pregnancy. Often already failing in school by the time they reach puberty, economically and culturally deprived adolescent girls have few prospects for a decent life. These teenagers are projected by the Sadkers to be 5 to 6 times more likely to become pregnant than are teens who are more affluent and successful at school. Why do these teens become mothers? According to Leon Dash,

> Some . . . girls were more afraid of birth control than of birth.
> Others bore children because they feared they were infertile.
> Some saw having babies as a woman's most important role, her
> primary purpose for being on earth. Others harbored terrifying
> histories of emotional, physical and sexual abuse. (In Sadker &
> Sadker, p. 116)

Undoubtedly, in some instances the low self-esteem experienced by some adolescent girls is caused by abuse, particularly sexual abuse. The incidence of sexual victimization among teen mothers is high and may contribute to premature parenthood (American Association of University Women Educational Foundation [AAUW], 1992).

Sexism and sex-role stereotyping play a crucial, if unacknowledged, role in creating the teenage mother. Western culture has honored the role of mother above all others for women. Thus, for some adolescents, motherhood is the ultimate sex role and a way for a disadvantaged girl with few outlets to express herself, exhibit her talents, or win recognition to gain positive attention. Having a baby is a way for girls to gain love, to have something of their own, to demonstrate that they are "mature" and therefore to be respected and heard, to be involved with someone—a child—who will not reject or abandon them, and most significant, it shows that they too can succeed at something. In the words of one of the teenage girls interviewed by Constance Willard Williams, "I told myself, *wow*, I'm a mother! I was happy; I was excited; I was really totally excited. I was shocked; I was surprised. Like wow, I really have a baby" (in Sadker & Sadker, 1994, p. 117).

Bottom Line for Administrators

Given the powerful social, psychological, cultural, and economic factors contributing to a perceived crisis of teenage pregnancies, school officials can feel ill-equipped to assist and uncertain of where to begin. Being aware that teenage pregnancies often relate to low self-esteem is a good place to start. Administrators and teachers can focus on ways to counteract low self-esteem with the tools they have available. For instance, Rauchelnekave (in Sadker & Sadker, 1994) concluded that unidentified and untreated learning disabilities that resulted in school failure were "a hidden but powerful motive for teen pregnancy and birth" (p. 118). Because girls are less likely than boys to be identified as having disabilities, they are less likely to receive special education services. Girls with learning disabilities remain in the regular classroom where their silence and reluctance to participate sets them up to fail. Recognizing this problem and giving adolescent girls, in particular those who are at risk for having low self-esteem, the opportunity to be heard and to succeed in the classroom from the very early grades are positive strategies for reducing the likelihood of teen pregnancies.

Counseling and Prenatal Care

Although a major goal of educators may be to reduce teen pregnancies, it is important that teens who do become pregnant receive counseling, health care services, and encouragement to continue their education. The importance of such an approach is that pregnancy is the leading reason that female students drop out of school. Nearly 1 out of every 10 teenage girls over age 14 gets pregnant, and more than half of all pregnant teens leave school prematurely (Weiner, 1987). The babies born to these teen mothers are at high risk for health problems and learning disorders that will continue to affect the schools when they are enrolled in future years.

Young adolescents' levels of physiological maturity are not matched by either their emotional or social development. They tend to be spontaneous, unrealistic, romantic, and incapable of anticipating rationally the consequences of their sexual behavior. They are not capable of identifying or appreciating the cost of premature parenthood. Therefore, if counseling programs are to be effective, they need to recognize and address this incomplete emotional and moral development.

A comprehensive program that addresses the needs of pregnant teens can reduce the drop-out rate for the pregnant adolescent, deliver comprehensive prenatal education to these students, and improve the health of teenage mothers and their children. We know that successful programs have kept teen mothers in school, reduced the occurrence of second pregnancies, and increased the mental and physical health and growth of both teen mothers and their babies.

Two vital elements to establishing successful pregnancy and parenting programs are an enthusiastic school staff and community health care services or organizations who will work in concert with the schools. Administrators who have made a commitment to schooling healthy children intuitively know how important the quality and nature of their staff are. Most principals, for instance, zealously guard their right to select faculty when hiring opportunities become available. They either directly (through carefully structured interviews) or indirectly (by following their instincts) choose the person who appears most congruent with the school's and the principal's goals or vision. Counselors and other service-related staff members must be chosen with the same care to ensure that their philosophical and ethical perspective concerning care for students synchronizes with the school's commitment to healthy children. They need to be informed with the latest information and to have the ability to seek out and connect with helping agencies that can assist students at risk for teenage pregnancy.

At the same time, counselors, teachers, and administrators also need to be aware of any liabilities that they may incur when handling pregnancy issues, yet not be unnecessarily inhibited in their work. As with educators, courts of law have not held counselors liable if they have used reasonable care in performing their job functions. Consequently, if counselors apply generally accepted standards of care and skill in working with teenagers, they are deemed to be acting reasonably and responsibly. However, it is important for counselors to be aware of any explicit school district policies prohibiting counseling related to birth control or abortion advice, or state policies or laws of a similar nature that could affect how they conduct their work. The best advice for counselors is to know and follow those laws and policies as well as the standard of professional behavior expected of competent counselors in their geographic area (Fischer & Sorenson, 1991). Generally, the constitutional right to privacy extends to minor children, but it is not absolute and not the same as adults'. According to Fischer and Sorenson (1991), some schools will refer students with questions, particularly those regarding abortion, to local health clinics, family doctors, and/or their parents.

In providing competent information about contraception or family services, the counselor is not behaving negligently under the law by referring students to federally funded clinics or services or those supported by state or local resources. However, if those actions are prohibited by local school board policy, then the counselor, although doing nothing illegal, may still be subject to disciplinary consequences from the school board (Fischer & Sorenson, 1991). Knowledge is the key.

In some school districts, as in Alexandria, Virginia, nurses are the primary counselors for students who become pregnant in Grades 6-12. These nurses can counsel students about all aspects of pregnancy, with the exception of abortion. Their main focus is on what occurs during pregnancy and what needs to occur after the baby is born. They also refer pregnant students to other agencies for information and assistance, including one that matches them with trained volunteer advocates, another that has good results with reducing child abuse and subsequent pregnancies, and a comprehensive clinic that provides counseling and health services.

Dealing With the Whole Family

Disturbingly, the literature gives little attention to the families of pregnant teens, although it is known that family structure strongly influences early sexual activity. Daughters in single-parent families are more likely to engage in early sex than girls who grow up in two-parent families because of the greater likelihood that there is less supervision in the home, less exposure to adults' sexuality as a normal part of life, and the lack of a father's steady affection and involvement. Girls whose relationship with their father has been severely damaged by divorce or whose parents have never been married are more likely than girls from intact families to engage in a quest for male approval and to seek love through early sex. Teenagers with older, sexually active siblings are more likely to begin having sex at an early age (Whitehead, 1994).

The adolescent is in a state of limbo: too young to be treated as an adult and too old to be treated as a child. The added complication of a pregnancy to an already tumultuous stage of life can make for a lonely and frightening experience. This is the time that adolescents most seriously need peer and parent support networks and other external resource systems. This is also the time, however, that existing informal support systems such as family, school classmates, or friends may deteriorate. For those adolescents who opt not to terminate a pregnancy and instead to raise the child, support networks are crucial to the teen's success as a parent and to the maintenance of a stable environment (Miller & Miller, 1983). Pregnant students who lack such support or who are alienated from it are abandoned at a time when they can least tolerate emotional isolation.

Not all adolescents come from supportive, caring homes. A pregnant teen's willingness to share decisions regarding her pregnancy with her parent(s) is based primarily on her perception of the quality of communication within her home and of how she thinks the news of the pregnancy will be received. Adolescents were most likely to disclose their pregnancies when a history of warmth, rapport, and decision-making involvement with their parents, particularly mothers, existed. A decision not to notify parents, or to notify only one parent (typically the mother), happens generally when the teenager comes from a family that is experiencing severe stress and dysfunction, or when a father is psychologically or physically absent from the home (Resnick, 1992). Several considerations for administrators and counselors become clear in these circumstances: First, counseling programs must factor in the dynamics of the adolescent's family when addressing issues of prenatal and postnatal care, and second, specific skills and knowledge must be acquired and used to deal with the emotional issue of teen pregnancy when working with families. Care and concern for the student, and respect for the family's dynamics as well as its values, are all part of a sound program.

Peer Relationships

Scott (1983) found that social and emotional peer pressures loom large among the forces propelling adolescents into sexual activity. "If everyone is doing it, then it must be all right" is how peers justify their behavior to each other. Peers tend to be more permissive than parents, and adolescents are influenced more by peers than by parents. The support that pregnant teens get from their peers varies across socioeconomic groups. As we have suggested earlier, teenagers from poor or deprived backgrounds, particularly teens who feel isolated and rejected, view pregnancy as a means of having someone to love. Their affluent counterparts are more likely to judge their pregnant condition as an embarrassment and consequently something to hide.

Peer counselors in clinics and prenatal programs have proven to be very effective in conveying important information regarding health care, nutrition, and child care as well as information regarding the prevention of subsequent pregnancies. Lee and Berman (1992) have pointed out that the nature of the care and support provided to pregnant teenagers is highly significant. Adult counselors, other important adults in the lives of pregnant teens, and peer counselors should strive to reflect care that emancipates, values, and respects the person being cared for. Care that is smothering or judgmental alienates the recipient from the provider, erodes the worth of the program, and defeats any objective the program may have to contribute to the maturation or self-sufficiency of the student. Pairing teens with other teens so that a close relationship can develop between them facilitates a process of sharing and learning on the part of all concerned. Peers are often a more welcome source of information and more successful than adult counselors in convincing adolescents to behave differently than they have in the past. Peer counselors who work with pregnant teenagers must be carefully trained, supervised, and supported in dealing with what sometimes can be stressful relationships.

Finally, teenage pregnancy programs must also address the teen father. After the baby's birth, teen fathers are usually left out of the loop of caring for or supporting their children. Although the consequences of early childbearing are more severe for girls, the effects on boys must also be considered. Recently, attention has been focused on how to ensure that teen fathers receive academic education, job training, and life-skills education to encourage their self-sufficiency and enhance their involvement with their child as well as their ability to assume financial responsibility for their offspring. Programs that help young fathers assume more responsibility for child care and support, although not necessarily encouraging marriage, are being viewed in some quarters as in the best interests of teen mothers and their children (AAUW, 1992). However, this is a controversial and ethical issue. Individual opinions are tied strongly to family and community beliefs and values as well as to the question of how the mother and child can receive the most constructive support.

The Student's Rights

Pregnant students' rights begin with the right to a free and appropriate education. First, the student has the right to continue with her education in the regular school setting. Although it is not uncommon for adults in educational institutions to feel uncomfortable or even disapproving when a pregnant teen attends school, it is imperative that administrators facilitate a welcoming environment that encourages continuance of the teen's educational process. Some teens may choose home schooling, an option provided by school systems for students who are unable physically to attend public school due to medical conditions. Also, some school districts provide alternative schools or programs specifically designed for pregnant teens in which they receive academic instruction in combination with prenatal information and child development courses. However, such programs are not mandated by law, and their availability varies on a district-by-district basis.

School officials do the student and the community a significant service when they work toward encouraging the pregnant student to remain in school before and after the birth, whether it is through supplementary programs that bolster the mothers' resolve, day care programs that tend to their babies while they are learning, or simply providing individual, caring attention. The cost of dropping the ball in this regard is very high, both in human potential and in economic costs to the local community and state. Sadker and Sadker (1994) report that slightly more than one fourth of teenage mothers aged 17 or younger will finish high school. For the almost three quarters who will not finish, the likelihood of obtaining jobs that will allow them to support their children varies from slim to none. These children are almost certain to be raised in abject poverty (female dropouts in 1990 earned $3,109 a year).

Full Service: The School as Broker

For children and teens who are at risk of failure or of becoming pregnant, the "one-stop," full-service school that provides comprehensive services delivered by a number of agencies—preferably in one location—is the best possible solution. A team of service providers, collaborating to meet the special needs of poor, neglected, isolated, unsuccessful, or culturally deprived adolescents, has a better chance of reducing the risks of a teen pregnancy.

School administrators wanting to initiate a full-service program or school in their district can look to models such as the New Beginnings program in Los Angeles or can begin to meet with community agencies to identify ways in which efforts affecting youngsters can be coordinated. Many states, such as Florida and Minnesota, are beginning to make incentive grant monies available for collaboration ventures between schools and other agencies serving at-risk children and adolescents. Recently, an office of the federal Centers for Disease Control and Prevention (CDC) has taken on the mission of supporting states financially when they make efforts to formalize, on the state level, interagency full-service cooperation toward improving the health and lives of children. Such initiatives can help to prevent broader problems and contribute generally to the reduction of teen pregnancy. Some individual full-service ventures offer services that range from training for parents to teenage pregnancy clinics, day care, health services, extended-day programs, tutoring, and drug abuse assistance (Curcio & First, 1993).

It is appropriate that school districts take a leadership role in brokering services for schoolchildren that will strengthen their academic, physical, mental, emotional, and moral health. They will need to proceed with sensitivity and work within the framework of the community; they cannot, however, allow potential conflict to keep them from exercising their own ethical responsibility to provide healthy schools for healthy kids.

HIV and AIDS in the Schools

Overview

It has been 13 years since AIDS was first identified as a medical phenomenon in the United States and 10 years since the virus that causes it, HIV, was discovered. Since then, HIV and AIDS have touched nearly every social institution and business enterprise in the nation, including schools. The disease has hit homosexual and bisexual men and intravenous drug abusers the hardest; however, some secondary and elementary school students have contracted the disease, and the incidence of seropositive students is rising. A 1987 report from the CDC indicated that at that time, the origin of nearly 95% of the reported cases of AIDS was the exchange of HIV-infected body fluids through sexual contact in both homosexual and heterosexual individuals and intravenous drug use. Because HIV in seropositive individuals (those who have tested positive for HIV) is present in some body fluids (primarily blood, semen, and vaginal secretions), actions that involve the exchange of these fluids between people greatly increase the chances of passing the virus from one person to another.

Since 1985, the risk of contracting AIDS through blood transfusions has diminished because blood is now screened by a test that can identify HIV antibodies. Although small amounts of HIV also have been found in saliva, tears, breast milk, and urine, current medical research indicates that with the possible exception of breast milk, the virus

16

cannot be transmitted through contact with these bodily fluids. Extensive studies have consistently found no apparent risk of HIV infection to individuals through close, nonsexual contact with AIDS patients.

It is clear that the major cause of the transmission of HIV and AIDS is through unsafe sexual activity and needle sharing, behaviors that can carry a high price without responsible and knowledgeable forethought. It is therefore absolutely imperative that students understand which behaviors put them at risk for HIV and AIDS, how HIV infection can be avoided, and that perilous consequences can result from irresponsible choices of action.

Employees and Students

School administrators increasingly have been faced with the reality of employees and students with HIV or AIDS. In some cases, the school community has reacted with fear, confusion, and even hysteria. Concern and care for these individuals is often greatly overshadowed by confusion regarding what procedures to follow, issues of confidentiality, and fear of the disease. Lack of knowledge and submission to pressure from parents and members of the school community have caused some school officials and school boards to make or support poor decisions in relation to their staff or students with HIV or AIDS. School officials must be prepared for the continued presence of students and employees with HIV or AIDS, understand the facts and the legal issues, and determine the appropriate response. Being prepared is the best way to help distraught parents, staff, or student groups.

Adolescents are at particularly high risk of contracting HIV. Statistics show that sexual activity increases dramatically during the teen years. By age 17, almost one half of all teenagers are sexually active. Research also shows that most teenagers do not use contraceptive protection. In a 1986 survey of 1,000 teenagers (cited in U.S. Department of Education, 1988), 53% of sexually active teenage boys did not use condoms. The incidence of teen pregnancy is linked directly to these figures.

Increased sexual activity among teenagers has resulted in higher rates of infection with other sexually transmitted diseases (STDs), such as gonorrhea, syphilis, and chlamydia (which is symptomless in females and can cause infertility if left untreated), and makes the transmission of HIV more likely. In addition, teenagers who are already infected with another STD have an increased susceptibility to HIV infection. Approximately 150,000 adults and young children have died of AIDS in the past decade, yet the reality of HIV and AIDS is not always acknowledged by adolescents who think it can't happen to them or that they are invincible and will not be affected. Adolescents live for the moment without the stream of experiences or full moral development that most adults have to draw on. Until that maturity becomes naturally available to them, they need wise support that will help them to make wise and moral choices; protection while they are learning to grow focused, emotionally independent, and healthy; and measures that prevent or reduce the possibility of contracting HIV. Some children's lives quite literally will depend on those measures.

Drug use also has been shown to be widespread among U.S. teens, though it is believed that only a small percentage of teenage drug users use intravenous methods. Sharing needles with someone who has HIV or AIDS can be ultimately fatal. When a student or employee becomes infected with HIV or develops AIDS, compassionate response to the person's needs can be eclipsed by suspicions regarding his or her lifestyle or habits. It is startling to see how swiftly a school community can shift its focus from helping the person with HIV or AIDS to allowing fear to reduce its response to name-calling and bias. It is important that school officials keep in mind the private and confidential nature of a person's HIV or AIDS status. If and when someone's HIV or AIDS status becomes public knowledge, administrators must focus on the real impact it will have on the school community and take steps to discourage rumors, slander, and innuendo. Conducting one's self within the boundaries of acceptable professional behavior means being nondiscriminatory, fair, and rational in carrying out the ethical administrative duty to maintain a safe and healthy environment for all.

State of Knowledge About HIV and AIDS

HIV is a retrovirus that attacks the body's immune system by penetrating the chromosomes of human t-cells that combat infection throughout the body. AIDS ultimately destroys the body's ability to ward off infection. Certain clinical criteria are necessary for a diagnosis of AIDS, and these criteria differ for men and women. Testing positive for the HIV antibody (being seropositive) is not the same as having the disease of AIDS. Depending on their symptoms, HIV-positive individuals may be

- Identified as an HIV carrier when the person is asymptomatic
- Diagnosed with AIDS-related complex (ARC) or a manifestation of lesser symptoms that range from swelling of lymph nodes and fever to serious neurological disorders
- Diagnosed with AIDS when the person manifests one of the serious medical conditions most often associated with a weakened immune system such as Pneumocystis carinii pneumonia or Kaposi's sarcoma

In 1986, the surgeon general of the United States concluded that there is no known risk of nonsexual infection in most of the situations we encounter in our daily lives. Specifically addressing the risk of transmission in the classroom setting, the surgeon general said that at that time no identified cases of AIDS in the United States were known to have been transmitted from one child to another in a school, day care, or foster care setting. Because such transmission necessitates the exposure of open cuts of one child to the blood or other body fluids of the infected child, it was viewed as a highly unlikely occurrence. Even if that exposure were to occur, routine safety procedures for handling blood or other body fluids would be effective in blocking transmission from an infected child to other children in the school. Casual contact between children and persons infected with the AIDS virus is not dangerous (U.S. Public Health Services, 1986). Subsequent research and studies have shown no evidence that there is any appreciable risk of transmitting the AIDS virus in the ordinary school setting.

School and Community Relationships

Due to the sensitive nature of HIV and AIDS, it is important that schools develop close working relationships with state and local public health departments to ensure that accurate, current, and complete information about HIV and AIDS is disseminated to parents, staff, and students. Information from "the experts" in the medical field has been known to dispel concern much more quickly than assurances from nonmedical school personnel. It is also essential that the school nurse be knowledgeable about safety precautions and appropriate procedures for children with HIV or AIDS. The nurse can be a vital link between community resources and the school.

The development of policies regarding the admission and placement of students infected with communicable diseases including HIV and AIDS should include input from health professionals, parents, school officials, and county or state health officers. School officials can take guidance particularly from court cases of the 1980s that interpreted Section 504 of the Rehabilitation Act of 1973 as protecting the right of students and employees with AIDS to be in the school setting, if they were "otherwise qualified" under the law to be there. Determination of such qualification is made on a case-by-case basis by a committee drawn from the broader school community and is based on concerns for the welfare of the individual child, as well as all the individuals in the school.

Confidentiality and Record Keeping

A number of states have passed laws that require reporting of HIV infection for public health purposes and also for maintaining the confidentiality of such information. The knowledge that a child or employee has HIV or AIDS can evoke fear from others who come in contact with them and may, in the case of employees, evoke condemning moral judgments. School administrators should be aware of the potential for social isolation should a child's HIV or AIDS status become known to others in the educational setting. School personnel and others involved in educating and caring for these children should be sensitive to the child's right to confidentiality and privacy. Confidential records must be maintained, and information regarding the status of an employee or student with HIV or AIDS should be disseminated only on a "need-to-know" basis to the administrators, teachers, school nurses, and public health officials involved.

How to Handle a Publicity Blowup

Unfortunately, there may be a time when confidentiality is breached and the word gets out that a staff member or student has

HIV or AIDS. The collective behavior of uninformed people can cause chaos and can be a most unpleasant situation for those involved. It is important that school officials be prepared for such a scenario.

There are several steps to take toward restoring order when hysteria erupts among students and the community. The following framework describes procedures to use when knowledge of a student or employee with HIV or AIDS is introduced into the school setting, fear takes over, and the situation begins to be chaotic. However, this framework is viable for any event that disrupts the educational process.

1. Respond immediately at the first occurrence of publicity. A single exaggerated article or news bite may be countered with an article containing the facts. Contact the media and insist on equal time to address the issue. A passive stance may incite further media misunderstandings.

2. Anticipate escalation, especially if the community has a history of reactionary behavior, the school has not dealt with such incidents directly or adequately in the past, or few people in the community are willing to intervene or help defuse the situation.

3. Follow school policies already formulated for dealing with perpetrators and supporting victims:
   a. Provide for a cool-down period.
   b. Insist on mutual respect and cooperation.
   c. Arrange for crowd control and dispersal.

4. Squelch rumors and provide updated information to the school community and the larger community on a regular basis.

5. Call in human relations support and ask appropriate community agencies to provide accurate information regarding infectious diseases. Make time, places, counseling services, and other human resources available to assist students, staff, and parents in expressing their fear, concerns, and feelings. A "town meeting" can be called to publicly address issues of concern.

6. Encourage student leadership, formal and informal, in finding solutions.

7. Follow up with strategies to prevent further incidents, such as parent education and workshops on HIV and AIDS.

8. Following the incident, determine what additional measures or resources may be needed in the school to eliminate the possibility of a recurrence (Curcio & First, 1993).

Precautions and Prevention

Knowledge is our best precaution against the spread of infection *and* ignorance. Every school program should provide a staff development component that includes the following:

- Clear and concise information regarding the characteristics of HIV and AIDS and how the virus is transmitted
- Legal rights of employees and students with HIV or AIDS
- Criteria for placement of students known to have HIV or AIDS
- Appropriate and safe procedures for addressing employee or student injuries that involve blood or bodily fluids
- Appropriate responses to parents (and students) who may be fearful regarding their children's exposure to other students with HIV or AIDS
- Sources of information and counseling regarding HIV and AIDS

Legal and Policy Issues

It is important that school districts have a legally sound policy and administrative regulations for dealing with HIV or AIDS and other communicable diseases. Because of the deadly nature of AIDS, parents are naturally concerned about their children's possible exposure to it. However, children and employees with AIDS also have rights and legal protections. Administrators, therefore, must consider carefully all decisions they make regarding seropositive students and employees. Specific laws have been applied successfully in cases where students and employees have argued for their right to stay in school.

- *The Education for All Handicapped Children Act of 1975* (P.L. 94-142) ensures that all children between the ages of 3 and 21 with physical, emotional, and/or intellectual handicaps are provided a free and appropriate public education in the least restrictive environment.
- *The Rehabilitation Act of 1973* was passed by Congress to provide protection for handicapped individuals in the workplace. *Section 504* of the act allows the exclusion of an individual only if there is a significant risk of communicating an infectious disease to others. The act very specifically defines a handicapped

person as any person who has an actual, recorded, or perceived physical or mental impairment that substantially limits his or her life activities.

- *The equal protection clause of the Fourteenth Amendment of the Constitution* prevents individuals from being excluded as a "suspect class" unless there is a compelling reason for the discriminatory treatment and no lesser alternative way to deal with the problem. Where a suspect class is not involved, a "lower tier" test would still require a rational basis for exclusion.
- *The search and seizure clause of the Fourth Amendment of the Constitution* prevents school districts from requiring mandatory AIDS testing for employees unless the request meets the Fourth Amendment test of reasonableness.
- *The due process clauses of the Fifth and Fourteenth Amendments of the Constitution* protect the liberty rights to privacy and reputation and the property rights of an individual. Proper notice and hearing must be given before these rights are deprived. An arbitrary and impulsive decision to terminate employees or exclude students from the school setting may deprive them of substantive and/or procedural due process.
- Common tort law provides at least three legal avenues that are potentially available to employees and students. *Defamation* may be claimed if untruths are written or said about students or employees. *Invasion of privacy* may be argued if truthful but embarrassing facts about a person are revealed. *Intentional infliction of emotional distress* has been recognized as actionable in some states. This last tort can be claimed by the student or employee who has AIDS and is forced additionally to deal with the upset of a public altercation.

In most cases involving students and employees with AIDS, the courts have been unanimous: Students or employees must be admitted to the school setting and treated as individuals without AIDS would be treated, where they are otherwise qualified. The courts also have been clear in their opinions regarding public school policy for the treatment of AIDS and other infectious disease issues. Schools must develop and adopt a clear and concise policy that addresses student admissions, student placement, staff development, and personnel policies.

Other Ways, Other Roads:
Gay and Lesbian Students

The rights and liberties that our founding fathers wrote into the Declaration of Independence and the Constitution were meant for all people. . . . It is time that our nation realized that a significant portion of our society is today excluded and that laws need to be written and enforced to ensure that lesbians and gays are not discriminated against in employment, public accommodations and housing.

BARRY GOLDWATER (1993, quoted in Bernstein, 1995)

The discussion of homosexuality is banned in many arenas, and yet the country is embroiled in a number of conflicts surrounding it, for example, whether lesbians and gay men have the right to serve their country in the military services. The struggles of lesbians and gay men against many forms of discrimination (in housing, employment, and education, as well as hate crimes) have resulted in litigation, ruined careers, recrimination, name-calling, fierce opposition, and fierce defense. Why is it that we, as a society, are so disturbed by homosexuality?

The reasons are many and complex. One reason is simply the age-old human distrust and fear of anyone who is different. Distrust of homosexuals is similar to prejudice against people whose race, gender, religion, or culture is different. Another reason is the strong emphasis American culture places on sex roles that imbues our judicial system and every other societal institution. However, at its base, this societal disturbance over homosexuality has to do with sex, a subject that conjures up taboos, confusion, fears, and repression even before the added factor of difference arises. Denial is often an easier road to take than confronting and overcoming one's fears.

A Search for Identity

Robert Bernstein (1995) describes with sensitivity and empathy what he imagines was his daughter's plight in growing up as a lesbian and trying to suppress her natural inclination toward homosexuality. From a young age, Bobbi Bernstein participated in sports and other "boyish" pursuits but denied her crushes on female classmates during her elementary school years. Her principal weapon in the struggle to quell her unwanted feelings was denial. Occasional thoughts that she might be gay triggered spasms of terror. Such an experience is not uncommon for young individuals who do not make a conscious decision to fall in love with members of their own sex.

Bernstein envisions the adolescent years his daughter suffered through, alone and terrified because she dared not share her feelings with anyone, least of all her parents. This is the lonely obstacle course many gay and lesbian kids have to negotiate without the support society automatically provides for their heterosexual peers. Growing up without parents, peers, role models, or supportive teachers to provide the essential feedback that says "You're all right" hurts—and it damages.

Richard Troiden (1989) describes four stages of homosexual identity formation. He bases his stages on repeated descriptions by lesbians and gay males of their recollections of how they acquired homosexual identities.

1. Stage 1 is *sensitization,* and it occurs before puberty. As adolescents, most lesbians and gay males view themselves as heterosexual if they think about their sexual status at all. Despite questionable feelings and peer name-calling (tomboy, sissy, etc.), few see themselves as sexually different before age 12 or labeled themselves as homosexual at this stage.

2. Stage 2 is *identity confusion.* This occurs most typically during adolescence. Lesbians and gay males begin to acknowledge their difference at this stage and reflect on the idea that their feelings, behaviors, or both could be regarded as homosexual. At this stage, adolescents feel at odds with peers and cut off from others due to insufficient understanding of what they are experiencing. The emphasis on sex roles and the private nature of sexuality also compound their confusion and isolation. Adolescents may react to identity confusion with denial, therapy, efforts to form heterosexual relationships, avoidance, drugs, or acceptance.

3. Stage 3 is *coming out* to themselves. Typically, gay males define their homosexuality in terms of sociosexual contexts and pursue sexual relationships. Lesbians tend to emphasize feelings and minimize the importance of sexual gratification. The quality and type of initial experiences play a large role in reinforcing positive or negative attitudes toward homosexuality and in one's acceptance or rejection of that identity.

4. Stage 4 is *commitment.* This involves a feeling of obligation to follow a particular path or course of action. Commitment can be marked by entering a same-sex love relationship as well as by expressed satisfaction with a gay or lesbian identity. Disclosing one's identity to nonheterosexual others usually begins in this stage by coming out first to siblings or close heterosexual friends and later to parents, coworkers, or employers.

The Suicide Connection

The stages of homosexual identity formation as defined by Troiden make the process seem relatively simple and straightforward. However, the process can be a long and difficult one, frequently experienced in isolation and fear. First-person accounts of growing up gay almost always include periods of deep despair and suicidal thoughts.

Gay males and lesbians absorb from childhood the message—from some families, friends, schools, churches, synagogues, and the media—that homosexuality is evil. When adolescents begin to realize that they are lesbian or gay, they are hampered in accepting themselves by the same hurtful, internalized mental images of homosexuality that heterosexuals have. Many young people suffer years of hidden anguish, fear, and guilt before they come to terms with being gay or lesbian (Anderson, 1994). Fear of discovery can also be paralyzing and destructive to their sense of self. The need to hide, fear, and a lack of positive role models make the suicide rate among gay and lesbian adolescents 2 to 3 times higher than that of heterosexual youths.

Suicide is the leading cause of death for lesbian and gay adolescents in the United States. It has been estimated that they constitute 30% of all youth suicides annually. Many attempt suicide before the age of 17. Not only do gay and lesbian teenagers commit suicide in disproportionately high numbers, in their attempts to dull the pain; many also self-destruct more indirectly through the avenues of substance abuse or promiscuity.

Allowing Without Encouraging

It is important to understand what is known about sexual orientation. Recent research strongly suggests that sexual orientation—whether heterosexual, homosexual, or bisexual—may have a significant genetic component or may be strongly influenced by biochemical events prior to birth. Also, there is no adequate research to suggest that once established, a person's sexual orientation can be changed. Efforts to do so have been compared to changing handedness once left, right, or ambidextrous dominance is established: It may be possible, but it is also painful, psychologically damaging, and not natural.

It is important to keep this information in mind as we deal with the issue of homosexuality in our youths. Without encouraging a lifestyle, responsible educators can go a long way toward ensuring that school remains a safe and healthy environment for students struggling with their sexual identity. There are a number of ways in which we can communicate support. Many of these are steps that most responsible administrators already have taken to maintain a sound learning environment. They include the following:

- Providing appropriate responses to harassment of particular students because they are thought to be homosexual
- Selecting and hiring school counselors and other personnel with responsibilities in student services who have been trained to listen and work supportively with gay and lesbian students and who have skills in group processes to prevent disruption of the school system over a particular incident
- Educating the school community about homosexuality and adolescents
- Encouraging staff, particularly teachers, to be alert to signs of depression, cries for help, or other changes in behavior that may signal the possibility of suicide, and to take appropriate action by activating whatever resources the school has available, working with the family, and engaging local service agencies as resources

Finally, we take for granted that heterosexual adolescents' hormones will wreak havoc in the hallways and locker rooms of our middle schools and high schools and that we must do our very best to teach our heterosexual students responsible behavior and the art of good choices. So it is for gay and lesbian youths. They struggle with different choices, different feelings, and little peer or adult support, but their needs for love and acceptance are the same. Provide a mantle of support so that students are heard, but also provide accurate information about sexuality and sexual identity that allows all of them to make responsible and safe choices.

Parent Issues

She loved and accepted her child the way he was. In a perfect world, this would be the definition of "parent" in the dictionary. The point is not what you'll tell your friends at the bridge table. It is what you'll tell yourself in the end.

ANNA QUINDLEN, describing Jeane Manford,
the founder of P-FLAG
Cited in Bernstein (1995)

Psychiatric myths about homosexuals abound, as we have already suggested. In fact, the medical profession for years treated homosexuality as a personality disorder. The notion was fueled by early studies that looked only at gay men who had sought psychological counseling. The myths continue to receive credence by many nonprofessionals. Perhaps the most widespread misconception is that being gay stems from an unhealthy home environment, with the villains being a dominant, smothering mother and a passive or indifferent father. This theory has been discredited by medical research.

Many parents who are told that their son or daughter is gay react by saying, "Where did I go wrong?" as they try to understand what is happening to them and their family. Many believe their not sharing mother/daughter activities with lesbian daughters or father/son activities with gay sons is the root or cause. In the Broadway play *Twilight of the Gods,* the mother of a gay son tells him, "I must have dressed you funny. Or, I don't know, if only I hadn't taken your temperature that way." Guilt is only one of the emotions experienced initially by parents whose children have come out to them—anguish, sadness, fear, anger, concern, and confusion are others. Many parents pass through a series of stages very similar to the mourning process. In fact, they are grieving for the loss of the image and expectations they had for the child they raised.

Healing proceeds through stages of disbelief, denial, grief, and anger and ends, for most, in acceptance. The greatest difficulty is that parents feel their grief cannot be freely shared with others, and therefore they hesitate to disclose this deep dark secret. Some parents do not recover from the shock, treating their gay son or lesbian daughter as dead and excluding him or her from their lives. There are many stories of parents who throw their children out of their homes and never see them again.

Parents who wish to understand and maintain relationships with their children can be referred to support organizations such as Parents, Families and Friends of Lesbians and Gays (P-FLAG). This organization has branches in most large cities in the United States and provides a forum in which parents can talk, work through their grief, and share their innermost thoughts, concerns, feelings, and emotions with others who have "been there." Lesbians and gay men also attend these meetings in search of a means of communicating with their own families. Their attendance and participation quickly dispels the myths of homosexuality that many parents have held and helps them move toward greater acceptance of their own children. At P-FLAG meetings, parents meet gay and lesbian individuals who are simply men and women, both courageous and vulnerable, who confound all the stereotypes.

Development of Staff Attitudes

Acceptance of those who are considered different often begins with good models of acceptance. In the school setting, those models are the administrators and teachers who come in contact with students on a daily basis. Administrators must not only model tolerance, support, and acceptance themselves but facilitate this support from their staff as well. Education is the best means of teaching tolerance, disseminating the facts and knowledge necessary to eradicate ignorance, and providing the means to promote growth. To proactively include such education in many facets of the school setting, the following elements should be considered:

1. *Professional development.* Teachers, guidance counselors, nurses, psychologists, and administrators need to be educated about homosexuality. Professional development workshops can help accomplish this goal. Planned Parenthood, the Sexuality Information and Education Council of the United States (SIECUS), and P-FLAG are three of the best sources for up-to-date information.
2. *Support staff and services.* Staff members must be trained to deal with gay and lesbian students and issues of homophobia. Those responsible for the mental health of students in the school community must have current professional knowledge about homosexuality. Schools should be aware of local gay and lesbian resources, such as youth groups, gay and lesbian community centers, telephone hotlines, and organizations for parents.
3. *Sexuality in the health curriculum.* Some health textbooks mention homosexuality in brief, but it should be included in every discussion of sexuality, from dating to relationships to parenting. The social, psychological, and emotional development of gay and lesbian adolescents can be addressed right along

with that of their heterosexual classmates. Homosexuality should not be discussed only within the context of AIDS.

4. *Library.* The American Library Association maintains an active Gay and Lesbian Caucus. This group can be a source of information, book lists, and support for building an inclusive library collection. Fiction and nonfiction alike should reflect the presence of gay and lesbian people.

5. *Curriculum.* Gay and lesbian issues can be covered in the curriculum through professional development workshops. Teachers in different disciplines can discuss the lives and work of gay and lesbian individuals who have made important contributions, such as Langston Hughes, May Sarton, Willa Cather, Thornton Wilder, and Edna St. Vincent Millay.

Gender Respect: Antidote for Teasing, Harassment, and Violence

In a perfect world, respect for and fair treatment of others would be unconditional and not dependent on another's race, color, religion, national origin, or sex. In the less-than-perfect world we live in, there is a tendency to accept certain behaviors that promote ridicule and abuse of individuals as normal for children and adults. The teasing and harassing of girls about their bodies by boys is perceived as "just part of growing up" rather than a prelude to much more dangerous and violent behavior. Teachers' joking with students about sexual matters may be perceived as "just their sense of humor" rather than sexist and harassing behavior.

State and national surveys, studies, and court cases are confirming that sexist behavior and bias against female students at school are pervasive. They occur in varying forms in co-ed, single-sex, public, and private schools and in elementary, secondary, and postsecondary schools, causing serious harm to girls, boys, women, men, educators, parents, communities, and schooling (Curcio & Masters, 1993).

Boys and men are not always the harassers nor are girls and women the only ones harassed, but this is the most common and malignant pattern of sexual harassment. Boys are more likely to suffer sexual harassment if they do not conform to gender stereotypes, and much of the sexual harassment of boys is perpetrated by other boys (Shoop & Edwards, 1994). Same-sex sexual harassment is also a serious problem. More than 950 charges were filed by men in 1992, compared with 446 in 1989, and the number of sexual harassment complaints by men to the Equal Employment Opportunity Commission has more than doubled in the past few years. However, this is still only a fraction—roughly one tenth—of those filed by women.

Continuum of Offense: From Annoyance to Violence

Perception plays a major role in how people identify, label, and address behaviors. What one school official may perceive as harmless teasing, joking, or just "boys being boys," others may perceive as bullying, harassment, or abuse. A common understanding must be established as to which behaviors fall within the traditional realm of normal disciplinary issues such as pushing or verbal conflict and which behaviors constitute sexual harassment, abuse, or violence.

Sexual harassment is unwanted and unwelcome sexual behavior that interferes with a student's ability to get an education or to participate in school activities. "Unwelcome" means that the action is unsolicited and nonreciprocal. The person being harassed has not asked for or invited the behavior, nor has the person responded in kind with similar behavior. For example, wanted or reciprocal kissing, touching, flirting, or hugging is not sexual harassment (Shoop & Hayhow, 1994).

Behavior of a sexual nature refers to any action that has to do with sex. Actions can include the following:

- Using lewd or obscene language directed at an individual
- Making offensive sexual slurs
- Telling off-color jokes
- Spreading sexual rumors
- Writing and sending sexual notes or pictures
- Writing sexual graffiti
- Using sexist terms such as "babe," "toots," or "bitch"
- Using commonly considered terms of endearment such as "honey" or "sweetie"
- Referring to an individual's body parts physically or verbally
- Leering or ogling
- Unwanted touching such as hugging, pinching, kissing, or grabbing
- Pulling someone's clothing down or off

- Pulling your own clothes off
- Requiring sexual favors in exchange for special treatment or favors
- Attempting or committing rape

Some forms of harassment may also be crimes and punishable by law.

There are two important components to sexual harassment under the law:

1. *Quid pro quo* is a Latin term used frequently in the law. It means that if you do something for me, I'll do something for you. In the context of sexual harassment, quid pro quo may mean getting a better grade or receiving special treatment in exchange for granting sexual favors. It also can refer to negative treatment such as lowering a grade or refusing to write a letter of recommendation if the victim refuses to grant sexual favors. A single event can be used to establish quid pro quo in court.

2. A *hostile educational environment* is created by acts of a sexual nature that are sufficiently severe or pervasive to impair the educational benefits offered to the victim. A hostile educational environment is one that is intimidating to the reasonable student and interferes with the victim's opportunities to enjoy education in the same way his or her peers enjoy it. Interpreting the concept of "reasonable student" can be difficult because a man and a woman or a boy and a girl may perceive the same situation in different ways. The courts tend to favor the victim's point of view. However, the frequency, duration, repetition, location, severity, and scope of acts of the harassment are important components in establishing a hostile environment. There must be evidence of a consistent pattern of behavior.

Power and the Moral Responsibility

Sexual harassment is about power and control and the harasser's need to exert them over a victim. Economically, socially, and politically, harassment works to protect turf and provide a power differential—sometimes physical, sometimes psychological—that makes it difficult for victims to refuse unwelcome advances. Also, the sex roles that males and females learn to play early in life socialize them to rationalize sexual aggression and coercion on the part of males as permissible and their excuses for such behavior as acceptable ("She made me mad," "I spent a lot of money on the date," "She asked for it," etc.). In a teacher-to-student relationship, the potential for abuse of power exists because of the natural authority role of the teacher in relation to the student. Threats of lower grades or failure are a means of controlling or devastating a student.

Whether the harasser is an employee of the school system or a student, school officials have an obligation to recognize, address, and eradicate such behavior. Caring educators need to know what legal and other strategies are available and how to use them, not only to reduce a school district's liability but also to address the inequality and waste that harm everyone in the schoolhouse (Curcio & Masters, 1993).

As Bogart and Stein (1987) say:

> There is nothing innocent, normal, or funny about harassment. Sexual harassment should not be confused with flirting, which is often welcomed and reciprocated and which, in any case, the recipient is free to ignore; nor is it seduction, which the recipient can stop by not responding. . . . Sexual harassment is unwelcome sexual attention that a victim is powerless to stop, and, as such, it may be better conceptualized as an act of aggression than as a sexual act. (pp. 146-147)

Administrators must learn how to tell the difference between sexual harassment and other kinds of behaviors requiring disciplinary action and address these behaviors expediently and with effective consequences.

Peer-to-Peer Harassment

The newest form of sexual harassment the courts have recognized is peer sexual harassment. Incidents of unwelcome verbal and physical sexual harassment of girls by boys in elementary, middle, and high schools are occurring with increasing frequency. When schools do not take steps to stop peer sexual harassment, they may be liable to their students.

A San Francisco school district and its principal were sued by an eighth-grade student for unchecked peer harassment when the student alleged that boys made obscene references to her breasts and other body parts and repeatedly called "moo moo" whenever she was in their presence (cited in Shoop & Edwards, 1994). The school district settled by paying the student $20,000. A Minnesota school district settled a case for $15,000 after failing to remove graffiti that referred to a student as a "slut" and made other sexual commentary about her (cited in Shoop & Edwards, 1994).

Peer sexual harassment also occurs in elementary schools. In Eden Prairie, Minnesota, the parent of a 7-year-old girl filed a complaint with the U.S. Department of Education's Office of Civil Rights (OCR) after school officials failed to put a stop to repeated harassment of her daughter on the bus, in the classroom and hallways, and on the playground (U.S. Department of Education, OCR, 1993). The harassment was in the form of name-calling and unwelcome touching. In May 1993, federal investigators concluded that the child's civil rights were violated by the school district's failure to take appropriate action to alleviate a "sexually hostile environment." They further found that the district did not establish culpability or forcefully discipline any of the students believed to be involved in the harassment. OCR rejected the argument that some of the harassers were special education students and therefore exempt from punishment due to their handicapping conditions. Under Title IX of the Education Amendments of 1972, a recipient (of federal funds) may not act any less effectively to combat sexual harassment by special education students than by regular education students. Although there was no monetary settlement, the district did enter into an agreement with the federal government to be more prudent in addressing sexual harassment. The Eden Prairie case points to the fact that the OCR believes that an educational institution's failure to take appropriate action for peer sexual harassment it knew of or had reason to know of is a violation of Title IX.

A middle school student in California sued the Petaluma City School District in federal court after she alleged that school officials failed to stop pervasive sexual harassment by her peers over a 2-year period. Specific complaints included students, both male and female, calling her "hot dog" and claiming she had sex with hot dogs, and daily graffiti on the bathroom walls referring to her alleged sexual prowess with hot dogs. Repeated requests for action on the part of school officials was met with comments such as "boys will be boys" and "it's a phase that will pass." The student's parents eventually moved her to a private school. The courts found that a hostile educational environment did indeed exist; however, in this case monetary damages were not awarded due to lack of clear proof that the employees of the school discriminated against the students on the basis of sex. This is a case we are likely to hear more about.

The number of cases alleging sexual harassment between peers is increasing, and although the boundaries of the liabilities of school officials have not been clearly established, it is definitely an issue before the courts. School officials can practice preventive law and strong leadership by exercising zero tolerance of student-to-student harassment.

Student-to-Teacher Harassment

We may assume that because of their age, education, maturity, experience, authority, and status, teachers always hold the power in teacher-student relationships. However, teachers also report being embarrassed, degraded, undermined, and humiliated by students. In most cases, the victims are female teachers (Shoop & Edwards, 1994).

Sexual harassment of teachers ranges from physical intimidation (i.e., a group of male students surrounding a female teacher at her desk and barring her exit) to suggestions from male students that they would be happy to "service" female teachers. Teachers have endured obscene phone calls, comments about their bodies and sex lives, and obscene gestures. Situations like these need to be dealt with directly so that they do not escalate into graver assaults, and so that school leaders communicate to students and staff their determination to stem all forms of assaultive or discriminatory behavior.

Teacher-to-Student Sexual Abuse and Harassment

Teachers and students theoretically and morally are prohibited from any sexual contact on the basis of teachers' professional obligation to act in place of the parent (*in loco parentis*) while the child is in the care of the school. Therefore, the relationship between school employees and students is a special one that may hold school employees to a higher standard of care under the common law than are many other employees (Curcio & First, 1993). In general, this trust is valued and honored; when it is broken, the costs are not only moral but legal.

One of the greatest betrayals of students by a teacher or administrator is that of sexual harassment, assault, abuse, or rape. Despite the outrageousness of such behaviors, they are not uncommon, according to court cases, research studies, and anecdotal records documenting sexual assaults of students by school employees. During the spring of 1993 in Union Springs, New York, police in the same week charged two teachers with sexually abusing children (cited in Graves, 1994). A popular sixth-grade science teacher was arrested for molesting children and trafficking in child pornography, and a high school music teacher resigned after former female students charged he had sex with them. Both teachers had been in the classroom for more than 2 decades.

Recent cases have sent a clear message to school officials that it is risky to ignore complaints of sexual misconduct involving school employees and students. In a Pennsylvania case, a young woman claimed that the school district had a constitutional duty to protect her from the sexual advances of her band instructor (*Stoneking v. Bradford Area School District*, 1987). When the U.S. Supreme Court ordered the 3rd Circuit Court of Appeals to rehear the case, the new ruling was that school administrators can be held liable for the actions of the offending teacher because they have direct supervisory control over that teacher's actions.

In another case, a superintendent and principal appealed, seeking immunity from a suit filed by an abused high school student in Taylor, Texas (cited in Graves, 1994). The girl charged that the principal ignored abundant evidence, including complaints from other teachers, that a teacher had used his position to form a sexual relationship with her. In March 1994, the U.S. Court of Appeals for the 5th Circuit (*Doe v. Taylor Independent School District*, 1994) ruled that students have a constitutional right to be protected from sexual abuse at school and that administrators can be held personally liable for neglecting to protect that right.

The Civil Rights Act of 1871 (42 U.S.C. § 1983) holds a person acting on behalf of a school district liable for violation of any "rights, privileges, or immunities" secured by the federal constitution or laws. The courts have held that a student has a federal constitutional right to bodily integrity and that school administrators owe a duty to students to prevent sexual abuse by school employees. In a recent case, the U.S. Court of Appeals held that a principal could be liable when he ignored a series of rumors and reports about a teacher who was having sexual intercourse with a student. The court said that supervisors are liable for "deliberate indifference" to constitutional violations by subordinates. The court found:

1. The administrator had learned of facts or a pattern of inappropriate sexual behavior by a subordinate pointing plainly toward the conclusion that the subordinate was abusing the student.
2. The administrator demonstrated deliberate indifference toward the constitutional rights of the student by failing to take action that was obviously necessary to prevent or stop the abuse.
3. The failure caused a constitutional injury to the student (McGrath, 1994).

A Highly Significant Decision

Of even greater importance, and a strong warning to school boards and administrators of the dangers of ignoring or treating lightly students' complaints of sexual harassment by teachers, was the decision of the Supreme Court itself in *Franklin v. Gwinnett County Public Schools* (1992). Beginning in the 10th grade, Christine Franklin was subjected to continual harassment and coercive sex by a coach and teacher, Andrew Hill, without intervention from the school authorities. Incidents ranged from sexually oriented conversations to Hill's interrupting a class, requesting that Franklin be excused, and taking her to a private office where he subjected her to coercive intercourse. Perhaps most shocking to concerned parents and educators was the information that school officials became aware of and investigated this harassment but took no action to stop it. In fact, Franklin was discouraged from pressing charges against Hill. The Court found that student plaintiffs can bring suits for monetary damages against school officials under Title IX of the Education Amendments of 1972. Until this case, it was not believed that monetary damages could be recovered under Title IX; the decision added support and impetus to the press against sexual harassment.

Sexual harassment, assault, and abuse by employees in the public schools are forms of sex discrimination prohibited under criminal child abuse statutes, criminal rape statutes, other criminal sanctions, the Fourteenth Amendment, Title VII of the Civil Rights Act of 1964 (amended in 1972), Title IX of the Educational Amendments of 1972, the 1991 Civil Rights Act, state fair-employment practices, and state laws modeled after Title IX. In addition, state regulations of the conduct, licensure, and certification of administrators and teachers may also come into play. Prosecution of abuse under one of the first three categories is a criminal proceeding that can result, if convicted, in imprisonment and fines. Suits brought under Title VII and Title IX allow for monetary compensation to the victim and penalties to the school, whereas enforcement of state licensure and certification regulations can remove a teacher both from a particular school district and from licensed teaching altogether.

Clearly, the courts view sexual misconduct of school employees involving students as serious, and their sanctions are severe. These decisions may well spur many future lawsuits against schools for the sexual misconduct of school personnel.

Mandatory Reporting

Historically, few districts have outlined procedures for reporting allegations of sexual abuse by staff members or established policies for dealing with allegations once they were made. Many districts develop policies at the time they are needed or in the aftermath of an incident. It is imperative that school districts deliver a strong message to employees and students that sexual harassment and abuse will not be tolerated, that all incidents must be reported, and that reported incidents will be addressed expediently using appropriate measures. Districts that have fewer incidents of sexual abuse have at least three things in common.

1. They have in place strong and clear policies on sexual harassment.
2. They make sure all employees and students know what these policies are and know how to make complaints.

3. They educate students and staff members about sexual harassment and about what to do if harassment occurs.

School staffs in these districts are aware of possible signs of sexual harassment and speak up when they see evidence suggesting possible abuse of a student. Complaints are taken seriously.

Investigations are best handled by a trained investigator. This means that the district should either turn the investigation over to the local police, hire a private investigator who has experience investigating child sexual abuse, or work with intermediate agencies to set up a special unit within the region or state to deal with allegations of sexual abuse of students by staff members. Quick action is important so that all individuals involved (the accused and the accuser, parents, witnesses, etc.) can be interviewed and the accused employee removed from contact with students during the investigation.

Although the district policy and procedures will outline the schools' individual reporting mechanisms, the policy should require that all allegations of staff-to-student sexual harassment be transmitted to the superintendent or to a special unit assigned to investigate such matters. In the case of serious allegations such as abuse or rape, administrators should not keep quiet nor they should they handle the investigation themselves. Reports should be turned over to the police or the department of social services. Administrators are responsible for creating a climate that is hostile to sexual abusers and supportive of those who report them (Shakeshaft & Cohan, 1995).

Parental Education

Our students' first teachers, their parents, must also understand the nature of sexual harassment. Parents have many of the same misperceptions regarding what aberrant behaviors are and what normal development is as those expressed by school officials. They may see many "boy" behaviors as normal because it is what they experienced growing up. Parents must be educated regarding the characteristics of sexual harassment and the consequences of such actions. Schools and parent-school organizations can be a vital part of this education by taking the initiative to singly or jointly provide workshops or seminars, speakers, and materials, as well as one-to-one discussions when appropriate.

Staff Development

All staff members and students need more than a single session of sexual harassment training. This topic, as do many others, requires follow-up, with time allowed for reflection, discussion, and asking questions after the basic information has been given.

Annual training sessions ensure that new staff members are trained. Training sessions should define sexual abuse and harassment, present examples of behaviors that are not allowed, and help employees and students understand the district's sexual harassment policy and complaint procedures. Staff members must learn how to help students talk about the issues of sexual harassment and how certain language and behavior by staff members can stop students from telling them their stories.

Districts also should teach students about inappropriate behavior by adults and where to report it if they see it. However, district leaders need to be wary of becoming so ardent in their war against child sexual abuse that they make teachers afraid to hug children and children so uneasy about touching that they interpret a warm and innocent arm around the shoulder as abuse (Graves, 1994).

Legal and Policy Issues

Sexual harassment is illegal in schools, and students and school employees are legally protected against sexual harassment. Victims, or advocates acting on the victim's behalf, can file sexual harassment complaints. It is critical for schools to be prepared to respond to concerns responsibly and in accordance with relevant law. Therefore, every district needs to adopt clear sexual harassment policies and effective complaint procedures that

- Are flexible enough to accommodate the varied situations that arise
- Contain formal and informal complaint mechanisms
- Identify several different persons to whom complaints can be brought
- Specify time frames for bringing, investigating, and resolving complaints, and prohibit retaliation

- Do not promise absolute confidentiality, but state that confidentiality will be protected to the extent that the investigative process allows

Under the legal doctrine of *respondeat superior,* a school district is responsible for unlawful acts of its employees that occur in the course and scope of employment but not for actions employees take for their own purposes. Sexual abuse of students generally has been held to be outside the course and scope of employment, even when committed on school grounds or while engaged in school-related activities. However, administrators may be legally responsible for their own action or inaction in these cases. State courts often award monetary damages in cases involving various administrative duties, such as

- Failure to supervise
- Failure to train
- Failure to warn or investigate
- Failure to report child sexual abuse
- Failure to hire carefully (McGrath, 1994)

For the Good of All:
Sex Education

Although moving and powerful arguments have been and continue to be made for keeping sex education essentially private and familial, waves of STDs, startling increases in teenage pregnancy, and the growing incidence of AIDS in young people have combined to keep sex education more or less a part of the public school curriculum in recent decades. The statistics on teenage pregnancy and estimates on the numbers of teenagers who have contracted STDs have provided powerful reasons to educators and other agency personnel to try to reach kids with sex education before they become sexually active (Black, 1995). In recent years, the trend in public approval of sex education programs for adolescents has been upward, counter to the popular belief that the public is increasingly opposed to these courses.

Whose Responsibility?

Once upon a time, mothers and fathers sat down with their daughters or sons and embarked on the thorny tale of "the birds and the bees." Mothers told the story to prepare their daughters for the onset of menstruation and only touched lightly on the fact that this was a threshold experience that can lead to the state of motherhood. The discussion of "hygiene" and needed accessories was punctuated with vague warnings to stay away from the boys. Fathers had similar, although shorter, conversations with their sons, which could be summarized like this: "Now don't get anybody in trouble." Thus the troublesome subject of sex education was covered.

Times have changed and so have approaches to sex education, although many still cover it the old-fashioned way and would like things to stay that way. Others leave their children's sex education to peers, the streets, or the schools. The issue of who should be responsible for teaching children about sexuality is a hot topic with as many facets as a fine gem. Who should teach it? What exactly should be taught? How should it be taught? Must it be taught?

Children must be educated by caring persons regarding sexuality, and that education must be comprehensive. If parents do not or will not undertake this responsibility, then the schools must assume it in the same way that they have assumed responsibility for educating about drugs and hygiene. We have moved beyond the issue of whether it is necessary; we know it is imperative, given the dangers to students of ignorance. Although the AIDS scare primarily is what has brought sex education back into the controversial spotlight, the growing problem of teenage pregnancy also provides a well-publicized, good reason to make these programs as available and comprehensive as possible. Such availability and comprehensiveness are best assured by state-mandated curricula.

Religious Concerns Versus State's Obligation

Some parents have deep religious concerns about sex education in the schools. When parents have objected through the judicial system to sex education courses as a violation of their First Amendment rights, courts have declared that the only substantial constitutional issue involves the free-exercise clause, that is, such compulsory courses may undermine the family's free exercise of its religion. The courts have rejected claims that sex education or family life programs constitute an establishment of religion. They have also rejected claims that sex education establishes a state morality or a religion of secularism and have found sex education to be in the nature of a public health measure (First, 1992). However, the right to free exercise remains an issue for some families who see sex education as usurping parental authority.

However, states have made efforts to accommodate parents on the matter of the free exercise of religion. In the majority of cases, school-parent conflict may be avoided through state laws that permit parents to withdraw their children from sex education classes because of religious objections (commonly known as the *excusal option*). Although both states and individual school districts try to keep the use of excusal options to a minimum, it has been the compromise of choice in other areas of dispute, for example, in deciding which books are taught in a reading class. It is important to note that the excusal option is a policy determination of state and local school boards. However, courts have supported sex education courses even where an excusal option was not present (First, 1992).

Clearly, the notion of state imposition of sex education curricula raises broader issues regarding the inculcation of values in the public schools. The question of who decides what to include in sex education curricula is obviously controversial. Basic questions to ask are Which civil virtues are properly civil? and Which ones are best left to religion? These are the kinds of questions that are being argued before the courts, but their resolution probably belongs more appropriately within a school or school district and its community. These are volatile issues, but a patient and courageous set of educators and school community can go a long way toward consensus by working through the issues among themselves.

Complaints and Outrage

The public nature of sex education as it is taught in schools is a red flag for parents who want their home life to remain private and sacred. Because class assignments may directly involve students in discussions of their own conduct and attitudes, religious and moral questions are immediately invoked. As a result, questions of privacy and of parental control also arise (First & Rossow, 1991).

Those who would have sex education stricken from every school curriculum cite the failure of sex education to accomplish what its advocates claim it will do. Detractors maintain that comprehensive sex education places its faith in the power of knowledge to change behavior; yet the evidence overwhelmingly suggests that sexual knowledge is related only weakly to teenage sexual behavior.

Whitehead (1994) describes the work of researcher Douglas Kirby of ETR Associates, a nonprofit health education firm in Santa Cruz, California, who has studied sex education programs for more than a decade. During the 1980s, he conducted a major study of the effectiveness of sex education programs for the Department of Health, Education, and Welfare, and he has since completed a study for the CDC on school-based sex education programs designed to reduce the risks of unprotected sex. His research shows that students who take sex education courses do know more about such matters as menstruation, intercourse, contraception, pregnancy, and STDs than students who do not. But more accurate knowledge does not have a measurable impact on sexual behavior. He found that ignorance is a problem, but knowledge is not enough to become the solution. Haffner (in Black, 1995), however, cites research showing that students who take part in cognitive-based lessons that are combined with affective-based lessons "are more likely to maintain abstinence and to use contraception when they become sexually active" (p. 39). Giving students just the biological facts sends the wrong message, Haffner thinks. They also need to be instructed on love and affection, caring and commitment, and decision-making skills that would strengthen their ability to choose abstinence.

Some supporters of sex education believe that sex education works best when it combines clear messages about behavior with strong moral and logistical support for the desired behavior. Therefore, in their view, formal sex education is most successful when it reinforces abstinence among young adolescents who are already abstinent.

Choosing the Curriculum

Comprehensive sex education is not just a movie about menstruation and a class or two in human reproduction. It should begin in kindergarten and continue into high school, sweeping across disciplines, from the biology of reproduction, the psychology of relationships, and the sociology of the family to sexology. Ideally, sex education should encompass sexual knowledge, beliefs, attitudes, values, and behaviors. Classroom instruction should address anatomy, physiology, and biochemistry of the sexual response system; sex roles; identity and personality; and thoughts, feelings, behaviors, and relationships. Students should discuss and debate ethical and moral concerns and group and cultural variations. At its best, sex education is about helping to create a world where all people have the information and the rights to make responsible sexual choices without regard to age, gender, socioeconomic status, or sexual orientation (Haffner, in Sears, 1992, p. vii).

Realistically, not every topic that should be included in an ideal curriculum will be freely accepted by all. Modern sex education courses sometimes include sensitive subjects such as contraception and abortion. The popular press has labeled abortion the subject that splits the nation as deeply as did beliefs about slavery just before the Civil War. Thus it is no surprise that discussion of these subjects in sex education courses is controversial. Involvement of the community by school officials in the development and content of sex education programs seems to be a crucial factor in minimizing controversy, even if nothing can fully eliminate it. In addition, a broadly defined state-level policy can leave room for local districts to devise their own curriculum locally, thus responding to community needs and reflecting community values.

The development of a broad-based community support network is the factor most discussed in the literature on the subject of sex education curriculum development. Some state policies mandate community participation in the development of local policy. The New Jersey state policy, for example, mandates that communities form advisory boards that include teachers, school administrators, parents and guardians, pupils in Grades 9-12, community members, physicians, and members of the clergy. In a curricular area as sensitive as sex education, it is important that there be vehicles for community comment so that parents feel that they retain some control over their children's lives and futures (First & Rossow, 1991).

Important questions that should be addressed in developing a sexuality curriculum include the following:

- What sexual knowledge is of most worth (and consequently, what is to be included or excluded in the sex education program)?
- How do educators incorporate that knowledge into the school curriculum?
- How do students interpret it?
- Who has access to what types of sexual information?

Another piece of good policy development is building an evaluation system into the program at the very beginning of program planning. This will force precision in the goal setting for the program and assure those who may be doubtful of the program's merits that there will be a *point of accountability*.

Of course, the curriculum itself must be based on effective teaching strategies that relate subject matter to students' interests, needs, and experiences so they are able to attach personal meaning to what is learned. From this perspective, curriculum is better assessed on the basis of personal development and experience rather than artificial goals and a scope and sequence chart.

Providing comprehensive sex education is a large task. School officials are responsible for working with staff, students, and parents to implement a program that will address the issues and alleviate the problems that threaten to undermine children's safety and well-being. Time should be taken to examine with the entire community which values and beliefs are uppermost before designing or adopting a program, or deciding on its goals or purposes. The differences among the various models should be explored and the right one for the school community should be chosen (Black, 1995).

Who Teaches It?

Deciding who teaches human sexuality is as important as the selection and development of the curriculum. As is true in any subject matter, the teacher who relates well to students will be the teacher who effectively communicates the curriculum to them.

Sapon-Shevin and Goodman (1992, pp. 101-104) provide a picture of who should teach sex education in their description of Ursina, a science and art teacher in an independent middle school in Bloomington, Indiana. Ursina designed instruction on a foundation of democracy and progress. She thoroughly addressed biological information regarding adolescent development and reproduction from an antisexist perspective, embracing social and psychological themes. These included allowing student expression, helping students appreciate their bodies, exploring the dynamics of human sexual relationships, and addressing the potential problems of adolescent sexual behavior and potential pregnancy. She set the stage of each class with ground rules needed to facilitate communication.

1. Anything that is said by any student during class is confidential.

2. There are no "stupid" questions and no one should laugh at anyone else. Each student has a different knowledge base and everyone needs to respect each other no matter what information or misinformation they might have.

3. No one may ask a purposely "stupid" question in order to make fun of what is being discussed.

4. Students have the right to ask personal questions of other students, but the students being asked also have the right not to answer.

Ursina views education as a mutually constructive experience in which the teacher and students learn together; she is knowledgeable and dynamic and uses her talents and knowledge to help her students become more empowered and socially responsible.

Sex Education and the Critical Issues

Social and health problems, such as the spread of AIDS and the escalating teenage pregnancy rate, have turned the formerly private nature of sex education into a raging sociopolitical debate over public school curriculum and state versus local control in curriculum content decisions. At its base, this is a clash between contested interpretations of our cherished religious freedoms and the equally strong belief that there are times when government must intervene in local decisions for the protection of the "general welfare." In the age of AIDS, the general welfare depends greatly on successful sex education in the public schools (First, 1992).

Sex education in the schools has a significant relationship to the critical issues that plague our schools today: Large numbers of schoolchildren must cope with or face the possibility in their lives of teen pregnancy, HIV infection and AIDS, harassment and confusion over their sexual orientation, and sexual harassment or abuse. Other children who are fortunate enough not to have to face these problems must still cope with the complex stresses and rigors of adolescence and relationships with their peers. Today's students have less guidance because there are fewer caring adults present in the home environment, and those parents have less time to educate children "the old-fashioned way." If we are to make a difference and turn the tide against the forces that are threatening public health and stability, especially the health and stability of those who are society's most vulnerable members, we need to begin with education.

Comprehensive sex education programs, including but not limited to school-based clinics, are capable of reducing teen pregnancy rates. Study after study shows that sex education does not stimulate sexual behavior, and common sense tells us that knowledge leads to more responsible actions whereas ignorance produces irresponsibility. Fifteen percent of high school youths have had comprehensive sex education, whereas more than 55% have had intercourse by the time they have graduated from high school. There is evidence that youths who have had a sex education course are more likely to know about contraception, use it more regularly, and use the most effective methods (First & Rossow, 1991).

Children and adolescents also must understand the truth about HIV and AIDS—what they are and how they are related, how the virus is transmitted, and how HIV infection can be prevented. Knowledge, along with a proactive approach to education regarding HIV and other STDs, is the best solution to stemming both the spread of infection and the hysteria that sometimes result when parents, students, and staff are misinformed. Comprehensive sex education programs should teach students the facts and help them lead the way in practicing prevention, tolerance, and understanding. In addition, a truly comprehensive program must address gay and lesbian sexual orientation and not treat homosexuality itself as a disease. Harassment and abuse must also be addressed through education. Staff and students must clearly recognize the characteristics of harassment and understand that such behavior will not be tolerated.

Legal and Policy Issues

The courts in general have supported state and local school authorities in cases dealing with sex education programs. In one instance, for example, a court has upheld a state board of education regulation requiring that local districts provide a family life education program, including sex education for all elementary and secondary schools. Because the state requirement included procedures for exempting students whose parents objected to the program for religious reasons, the free-exercise and establishment clauses arguments were dismissed. In another instance, *Ware v. Valley Stream High School District* (1989), a New York State appeals court upheld a requirement that all students receive instruction on AIDS and alcohol and drug abuse. Citing protection of the public health and AIDS education as a compelling issue, the court placed educational interest above the exercise of "unbridled religious freedom."

Courts may sometimes specify content in a decision about the appropriateness of a course, but such examples are rare, as most courts are reluctant to intrude. However, in an Illinois case (*State of Illinois ex rel. Marcella Meyer v. Cronin,* 1980), the court advised the school and the state to include as part of the state's sex education policy and practice instruction on "abstinence from sexual activity and refraining from sexual intercourse as an alternative measure of pregnancy prevention whenever instruction is provided on methods of contraception."

The U.S. Supreme Court to date has declined to address broad challenges to sex education; other courts so far have basically supported sex education in the public schools. As communities all over the country consider sex education courses and interventions such as the distribution of condoms, they will have to weigh and balance many competing legal, moral, and policy demands. Religious beliefs versus public health issues, the right to privacy versus the right to knowledge and choice, the individual versus the state—all must be carefully considered, weighed, and judged (First & Rossow, 1991).

Final Words to the School Administrator

The purpose of this book is to create a safe and healthy learning environment for students so that they may become productive and contributing people. Efforts to accomplish this sometimes conflict with the multitude of perspectives and values that represent the diversity of our communities across the country, whose needs educators are constantly trying to balance and accommodate. However, despite the difficulties, educators have ethical responsibilities of their own regarding the children whose education and welfare often rest largely in their hands.

Administrators have an ethical obligation to lead their communities in seeking solutions to the problems related to sexuality in schools today. It is important they join hands with parents, community, and other social agencies and institutions to do it. Remember, the ultimate challenge is to proactively create healthy communities containing healthy schools to educate healthy children who are neither perpetrators nor victims. In the process of dealing with this challenge, you will find that many resources are available to you, some of which have been mentioned in this book, and there are many persons in other agencies and in the community who are willing to support you. The task is large, the stakes are high, and the health of future generations of children hangs in the balance. If we are not a part of the solution, we are a part of the problem.

Annotated Bibliography
and References

Annotated Bibliography

Bernstein, R. A. (1995). *Straight parents, gay children: Keeping families together.* New York: Thunder's Mouth.

This personal account is by a father who came to terms with his daughter's homosexuality. Robert Bernstein tells about his own and others' experiences with P-FLAG, an organization that helps parents to achieve a fuller understanding and appreciation of human diversity.

Fischer, L., & Sorenson, G. P. (1991). *School law for counselors, psychologists, and social workers* (2nd ed.). New York: Longman.

In question-and-answer format, this book about legal matters, written for laypersons, is an invaluable pocket guide for anyone who does counseling in the public school setting. All of the major legal areas that are generally confronted in that setting are discussed—confidentiality, liability, privacy, abuse, drugs, testing, behavior control, disabilities, discrimination, and more. Each is discussed with an eye to practice rather than theory, and lots of specific incidents are included.

Sears, J. T. (Ed.). (1992). *Sexuality and the curriculum: The politics and practices of sexuality education.* New York: Teachers College Press.

> *Sears's book brings together curriculum scholars and developers with sexuality educators and sex equity specialists to explore the explicit and hidden curriculum of sexuality from kindergarten through college. This collection of 15 interrelated essays challenges conventional assumptions regarding sexuality and the curriculum while proposing specific curricular strategies and alternatives.*

Shoop, R. J., & Edwards, D. L. (1994). *How to stop sexual harassment in our schools: A handbook and curriculum guide for administrators and teachers.* Needham Heights, MA: Allyn & Bacon.

> *Administrators and educators at all levels who are working to create a harassment-free educational environment will appreciate this informative and practical handbook. Combining the expertise of an educational law specialist and an elementary school principal, it defines the problem, provides important background information, reviews the legal issues, and offers a specific plan for implementing a sexual harassment prevention program at the building level or in a school district.*

Shoop, R. J., & Hayhow, J. W., Jr. (1994). *Sexual harassment in our schools.* Needham Heights, MA: Allyn & Bacon.

> *This book gives the history as well as the legal and social context behind what far too many view as a normal problem in our schools. The authors provide valuable background and practical policies, procedures, and practices for parents and school leaders to use to develop a productive and friendly learning environment for all children.*

References

American Association of University Women Educational Foundation. (1992). *How Schools Shortchange Girls.* Wellesley, MA: Author.

Anderson, J. D. (1994). School climate for gay and lesbian students and staff members. *Phi Delta Kappan 76(2)*, pp. 151-154.

Bernstein, R. A. (1995). *Straight parents, gay children: Keeping families together.* New York: Thunder's Mouth.

Black, S. (1995). Sex and the public schools. *Executive Educator, 17(6)*, 38-41.

Bogart, K., & Stein, N. (1987). Breaking the silence: Sexual harassment in education. *Peabody Journal of Education, 64*, 146-163.

Centers for Disease Control. (1987, December 21). *AIDS weekly surveillance report*, pp. 1-5.

Curcio, J. L., & First, P. F. (1993). *Violence in the schools: How to proactively prevent and defuse it*. Newbury Park, CA: Corwin.

Curcio, J. L., & Masters, A. B. (1993). The broken silence: Sexual harassment of students. *People and Education, 1*, 223-232.

Doe v. Taylor Independent School District, 15 F.3d 443 (5th Cir. 1994).

First, P. F. (1992). Sex education in the public schools: A clash of religious freedom and the general welfare. *Educational Forum, 57*, 76-83.

First, P. F., & Rossow, L. F. (1991). Sex education in the public schools: Legal and policy ramifications. *Religion & Public Education, 18*, 259-268.

Fischer, L., & Sorenson, G. P. (1991). *School law for counselors, psychologists, and social workers* (2nd ed.). New York: Longman.

Franklin v. Gwinnett County Public Schools, 112 S. Ct. 1028 (1992).

Gilligan, C. (1982). *In a different voice: Psychological theory and women's development*. Cambridge, MA: Harvard University Press.

Graves, B. (1994). When the abuser is an educator. *School Administrator, 51*(9), 8-20.

LaCerva, C. (1992). Talking about talking about sex: The organization of possibilities. In J. T. Sears (Ed.), *Sexuality and the curriculum: The politics and practices of sexuality education* (pp. 124-138). New York: Teachers College Press.

Lawson, H. A. (1995). Schools and educational communities in a new vision for child welfare. *Journal for a Just and Caring Education, 1*(1), 5-26.

Lee, D., & Berman, L. M. (1992). Reconsidering teenage sexuality. In J. T. Sears (Ed.), *Sexuality and the curriculum: The politics and practices of sexuality education* (pp. 284-299). New York: Teachers College Press.

McGrath, M. J. (1994). The psychodynamics of school sexual abuse investigations. *School Administrator, 51*(9), 28-34.

Miller, E. K., & Miller K. A. (1983). Adolescent pregnancy: A model for intervention. *Personnel and Guidance Journal, 62*(1), 15-20.

Resnick, M. D. (1992). Adolescent pregnancy options. *Journal of School Health, 62,* 298-303.

Sadker, M., & Sadker, D. (1994). *Failing at fairness: How our schools cheat girls.* New York: Simon & Schuster.

Sapon-Shevin, M., & Goodman, J. (1992). Learning to be the opposite sex: Sexuality education and sexual scripting in early adolescence. In J. T. Sears (Ed.), *Sexuality and the curriculum: The politics and practices of sexuality education* (pp. 89-105). New York: Teachers College Press.

Scott, J. W. (1983). The sentiments of love and aspirations for marriage and their association with teenage sexual activity and pregnancy. *Adolescence, 18,* 889-897.

Sears, J. T. (1992). The impact of culture and ideology on the construction of gender and sexual identities: Developing a critically based sexuality curriculum. In J. T. Sears (Ed.), *Sexuality and the curriculum: The politics and practices of sexuality education* (pp. 7-33). New York: Teachers College Press.

Shakeshaft, C., & Cohan, A. (1995). Sexual abuse of students by school personnel. *Phi Delta Kappan, 76*(7), 512-520.

Shoop, R. J., & Edwards, D. L. (1994). *How to stop sexual harassment in our schools: A handbook and curriculum guide for administrators and teachers.* Needham Heights, MA: Allyn & Bacon.

Shoop, R. J., & Hayhow, J. W., Jr. (1994). *Sexual harassment in our schools.* Needham Heights, MA: Allyn & Bacon.

Stark, E. (1986). Young, innocent and pregnant. *Psychology Today, 20*(10), 28-30, 32-35.

State of Illinois ex rel. Marcella Meyer v. Cronin, Circuit Court of Cook County, No. 79L, 19607 (1980).

Stoneking v. Bradford Area School District, 667 F. Supp. 1088 (W.D. Pa. 1987).

Troiden, R. R. (1989). The formation of homosexual identities. In G. Herdt (Ed.), *Gay and lesbian youth* (pp. 50-68). Binghamton, NY: Harrington Park.

U.S. Department of Education. (1988). *AIDS and the education of our children* (4th printing). Washington, DC: Author.

U.S. Department of Education, Office of Civil Rights. (1993). *Letter of findings for Region V* (Docket No. 05-92-1174). Washington, DC: Author.

U.S. Public Health Services. (1986). *Surgeon general's report on acquired immune deficiency syndrome.* Washington, DC: Author.

Ware v. Valley Stream High School District, 545 N.Y.S.2d 316 (1989).

Weiner, R. (Ed.). (1987). *Teen pregnancy: Impact on the schools.* Alexandria, VA: Education Research Group.

Whitehead, B. D. (1994, October). The failure of sex education. *Atlantic Monthly,* pp. 55-80.

**CORWIN
PRESS**

The Corwin Press logo—a raven striding across an open book—represents the happy union of courage and learning. We are a professional-level publisher of books and journals for K–12 educators, and we are committed to creating and providing resources that embody these qualities. Corwin's motto is "Success for All Learners."